Creatures of the Forest Habitat

Skunks

Jackie Heckt

PowerKiDS press

New York

Published in 2017 by The Rosen Publishing Group, Inc.
29 East 21st Street, New York, NY 10010

First Edition

Editor: Caitie McAneney
Book Design: Mickey Harmon

Photo Credits: Cover (series logo) iLoveCoffeeDesign/Shutterstock.com; cover, pp. 1, 3, 4, 6, 8, 10, 12, 14, 16, 18, 20, 22—24 (background) BlueRingMedia/Shutterstock.com; cover (skunk), p. 22 Bildagentur Zoonar GmbH/Shutterstock.com; pp. 5, 7, 11 (inset), 19 (main) Geoffrey Kuchera/Shutterstock.com; p. 7 Gerard Soury/Getty Images; p. 9 Cynthia Kidwell/Shutterstock.com; p. 10 Yasmins world/Shutterstock.com; p. 11 (main) Holly Kuchera/Shutterstock.com; pp. 13, 17 critterbiz/Shutterstock.com; p. 15 S.J. Krasemann/Getty Images; p. 19 (inset) DnDavis/Shutterstock.com; p. 21 sattahipbeach/Shutterstock.com.

Cataloging-in-Publication Data

Names: Heckt, Jackie.
Title: Skunks / Jackie Heckt.
Description: New York : PowerKids Press, 2017. | Series: Creatures of the forest habitat | Includes index.
Identifiers: ISBN 9781499427165 (pbk.) | ISBN 9781499429268 (library bound) | ISBN 9781499427172 (6 pack)
Subjects: LCSH: Skunks–Juvenile literature.
Classification: LCC QL737.C248 H39 2017 | DDC 599.76'8–dc23

Manufactured in the United States of America

CPSIA Compliance Information: Batch #BW17PK: For Further Information contact Rosen Publishing, New York, New York at 1-800-237-9932

Contents

Stinky Skunks

What's the smelliest animal in the forest? That title goes to the skunk! Skunks are small **mammals**. They blast other animals with a stinky spray when they get too close. That's enough to keep most predators away!

There are more than 10 species, or kinds, of skunks throughout the world. That includes hog-nosed skunks, spotted skunks, and stink badgers. They come in many different sizes and colors. This book focuses on the striped skunk, which is the most well-known species.

Forest Friend Facts

The smallest skunk species is the pygmy spotted skunk. It's so small you can hold it in your hand!

Skunks often wander out of wooded areas and into neighborhoods. They love to go through people's trash.

5

Let's Find a Skunk!

Striped skunks are common creatures in North America. They're found in the warmer areas of Canada, across the United States, and as far south as Mexico. Other skunk species are found in Central America and South America.

American hog-nosed skunks live in the southwest United States and Mexico, too. You might get them confused with striped skunks, because they also have a stripe down their back. However, the American hog-nosed skunk has one thick, white stripe and the striped skunk has a white stripe that splits in two.

Forest Friend Facts

The Humboldt's hog-nosed skunk, or Patagonian hog-nosed skunk, has a bare nose that it uses to dig up insects and plants.

This striped skunk sniffs around in the grass. What do you think it will find?

A Skunk's Habitat

Skunks are very **adaptable** creatures. They live well in areas with many trees, such as forests and woodlands. They use the trees and other plants as cover or shelter. Skunks can survive in very cold weather and very hot weather, which allows them to live in many different areas.

Skunks don't just live in the forest. They sometimes live in grasslands and deserts. They're often drawn into cities and neighborhoods by the promise of food. They're commonly seen in parks and big backyards.

Forest Friend Facts

Skunks that live in cities and towns may make their home in old buildings or barns, or under porches.

Skunks sometimes use hollow logs as shelter. The forest is full of logs to live in.

Is That a Skunk?

You're out on a walk in the woods when, suddenly, a creature crosses your path. You think it's a skunk, but how can you know for sure?

Skunks are about the size of a house cat. They have a long, bushy tail. The best way to identify a skunk is to look at the pattern of its fur. Striped skunks have mostly black fur with a white stripe down their back. The white stripe splits into two in a "V" pattern.

Forest Friend Facts

Skunks have long claws that help them dig in the dirt for bugs.

Striped skunks have a very thin white stripe that runs from their nose to their forehead.

11

Skunk Families

During warmer months, skunks are solitary animals. That means they like to live and hunt alone. When the weather gets colder, however, some skunks come together in dens. They keep each other warm through the winter. Skunks also come together to **mate**.

A baby skunk is called a kit. A mother skunk usually gives birth to a litter of two to 10 kits each year. The kits are blind for about three weeks, and they depend on their mother to feed them and keep them safe.

These baby skunks may look cute, but stay far away. They can spray even before they can see!

Hungry Skunks

What does a skunk eat when it gets hungry? Skunks are omnivores. That means they eat both plants and animals. They will eat fruits and other plants they can find. They'll also eat small mammals, reptiles, and fish. These forest animals aren't very picky—they gladly eat trash and **carrion**!

A skunk's favorite foods are **insects**. They dig in the soil for baby insects, or larvae. They like to eat beetles, crickets, worms, grasshoppers, and many other bugs.

Forest Friend Facts

Animals that eat nearly anything that's available are called opportunistic eaters.

This skunk is very brave.
It's clawing at a wasp's nest.
Hopefully he won't get stung!

A Smelly Defense

A skunk's liquid spray is called musk. It's the best defense this forest creature has! The smelly musk comes from **glands** that are located at the base of the skunk's tail.

Skunks can spray their targets from up to 10 feet (3 m) away. They have great aim and usually shoot for the target's eyes. The musk hurts when it hits the animal's eyes, and it leaves the animal with a stink that can last for days. Luckily, skunks attack only if they feel **threatened** or if they're protecting their young.

Forest Friend Facts

You can smell a skunk's musk up to a mile (1.6 km) away.

Skunks usually give a warning before they spray. They pound the ground with their front legs. Then, they lift their tail and growl. That's a sign to back away!

17

Few Predators

North America has a very healthy population of striped skunks. That's because they're very adaptable to new habitats. Because of their defense, few predators attack skunks. They know the **consequences**!

Great horned owls are one of the few natural predators of skunks. They can attack from above the skunk, and they don't have a great sense of smell. Foxes, coyotes, and bobcats may try to hunt a skunk, but they will probably end up smelling for days.

Forest Friend Facts

Some people keep skunks as pets, but only after first having their musk glands removed.

great horned owl

Skunks are masters of their **ecosystem** because most other animals avoid them.

What Do You Do?

Skunks are shy animals. They usually only come out at night, and they like to be left alone. If you do run into a skunk, make sure to give it space. Back away slowly. Skunks usually give fair warning before they spray.

It's very important to keep your pets inside at night. Dogs can be curious, and that sometimes leads to them being sprayed by skunks. If your dog is sprayed, there are special products made to get rid of the smell.

Forest Friend Facts

Skunks can carry **parasites** such as ticks and fleas and diseases such as **rabies**. If a skunk bites you or your pet, go to the doctor or vet right away.

Washing your dog in regular water after a skunk attack only makes the smell worse.

21

Forests in Danger

Skunks are important to their ecosystem. They eat many kinds of insects, which keeps those populations in balance. Many insects are considered **pests**, and skunks are happy to get rid of them for us.

Striped skunk populations are not in danger at this time. However, their habitats *are* in danger. With forest habitats disappearing, animals such as the skunk have to move into neighborhoods and cities. It's important to save the forests and keep this stinky animal in its natural habitat.

Glossary

adaptable: Able to change in order to live better in certain environments.

carrion: A dead, rotting animal.

consequence: Something that happens as a result of a certain action or set of conditions.

ecosystem: A natural community of living and nonliving things.

gland: A body part that produces something that helps with a bodily function.

insect: A small, often winged, animal with six legs and three body parts.

mammal: A warm-blooded animal that has a backbone and hair, breathes air, and feeds milk to its young.

mate: To come together to make babies.

parasite: A living thing that lives in, on, or with another living thing and often harms it.

pest: An animal or bug that causes problems for people.

rabies: A deadly disease that affects the central nervous system. It is carried in the spit of some animals.

threatened: To feel afraid or nervous.

Index

B
bobcats, 18

C
carrion, 14
claws, 10
coyotes, 18

D
dens, 12
dogs, 20, 21

F
fish, 14
foxes, 18

I
insects, 14, 22

K
kits, 12

M
mammals, 4, 14
musk, 16

O
omnivore, 14
owl, great horned, 18, 19

P
parasites, 20
predators, 4, 18

R
rabies, 20
reptiles, 14

S
skunk, hog-nosed, 4, 6
skunk, pygmy spotted, 4
skunk, spotted, 4
skunk, striped, 4, 6, 7, 10, 11, 18, 22
spray, 4, 12, 16, 17, 20
stink badger, 4

T
tail, 10, 16, 17
trash, 5, 14

Websites

Due to the changing nature of Internet links, PowerKids Press has developed an online list of websites related to the subject of this book. This site is updated regularly. Please use this link to access the list: www.powerkidslinks.com/forest/skunk